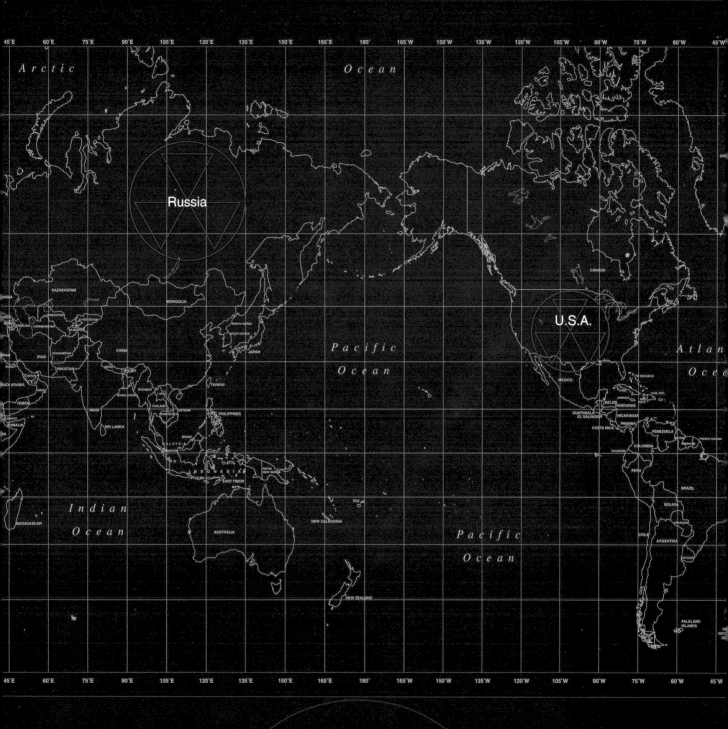

DAYS OF CHANGE

Creative Education

BY VALERIE BODDEN

Published by Creative Education
P.O. Box 227, Mankato, Minnesota 56002
Creative Education is an imprint of The Creative Company.

Cover design and art direction by Rita Marshall
Interior design and book production by The Design Lab
Printed in the United States of America

Photographs by Corbis (Bettmann, Hulton-Deutsch Collec-
tion, Seattle Post Intelligencer Collection, Peter Turnley), Getty
Images (2005 Laski Diffusion, AFP, Bettmann, Hulton Archive,
Time Life Pictures)

Library of Congress Cataloging-in-Publication Data
Bodden, Valerie.
The Cold War / by Valerie Bodden.
p. cm. – (Days of change)
Includes bibliographical references and index.
ISBN-13: 978-1-58341-546-7
1. Cold War–Juvenile literature. I. Title
D1058.B63 2007
909.52'5–dc22   2006019825

First edition
9 8 7 6 5 4 3 2 1

One of the great ironies of the Cold War was that both the United States and the Soviet Union dedicated massive sums of money—an estimated combined total of $8 trillion—to producing weapons that they hoped never to use. Under the theory of mutually assured destruction, nicknamed MAD, each country attempted to amass a nuclear arsenal capable of completely destroying the other, in the hopes that the other country would then be deterred from delivering the first strike in a nuclear war. While some today believe that MAD prevented nuclear war, others hold that it was only through sheer luck that disaster was averted.

Ballistic
Missile

Both U.S. and Soviet leaders feared that the Cuban Missile Crisis would end in nuclear war, but in November 1962, Soviet ships carried the country's missiles away from Cuba.

For 13 days in October 1962, people across America held their breath.

They had just learned that the Soviet Union had secretly placed nuclear missile installations on the island of Cuba, just 90 miles (145 km) south of the U.S. Each day, Americans watched the news, anxious for reports of the negotiations between the two superpowers. And each morning, they awoke wondering if that day would be their last. Finally, on October 28, Americans breathed a little easier. The Soviet Union had agreed to remove the missiles to de-escalate the conflict. They would live until tomorrow after all.

Those October days represented the heart of the Cold War, an intense rivalry between the democratic U.S. and the communist Soviet Union. For nearly 45 years, from 1945 to 1989, each nation sought to amass a huge store of nuclear weapons and spread its ideology across the globe. When the Cold War finally ended, the Soviet Union broke apart, and countries once under Soviet control were left trying to find their place in the new world order. At the same time, fears arose that terrorists might obtain nuclear weapons. Soon, people began to question whether the world had really been made any safer by the end of the dangerous U.S.-Soviet rivalry.

5

As World War II came to a close in 1945, the world was a very different place than it had been in 1939 when Germany, under dictator Adolf Hitler, had invaded Poland to spark off the conflict. Six years of intense fighting and massive bombing campaigns had reduced much of Europe and Asia to rubble, and more than 50 million people—both military and civilian—had been killed. Countries that before the war had been major powers—including Britain, Germany, France, and Italy—were severely weakened and exhausted by the conflict, and in their place, two new superpowers emerged: the U.S. and the Soviet Union.

FROM ALLIES TO ENEMIES

Of the countries most heavily involved in the war, the U.S. alone emerged stronger and more prosperous than ever. Since the war hadn't been fought on U.S. soil (aside from the surprise Japanese attack on the naval base at Pearl Harbor, Hawaii), American industry remained strong. During the war, the U.S. economy had doubled, as people across the country went to work manufacturing massive volumes of planes, warships, and other military necessities. When the war ended, the U.S. continued its high production levels, churning out more than half of the world's manufactured goods, including automobiles and home appliances.

South of the U.S., some of the countries of South America also fared well in the immediate aftermath of the war, in which most South American countries had supported the Allied nations of the U.S., Britain, France, and the Soviet Union. In Brazil, industrialization

The widespread fear of communism in the late 1940s and early 1950s gave rise in the U.S. to a period known as the Red Scare, in which the government sought to root out anyone with communist sympathies. At the forefront of the Red Scare was a U.S. senator named Joseph McCarthy, who accused several government officials of having communist ties. Those charged with being communist often lost their jobs, their money, and sometimes even their families. In Hollywood, too, hundreds of writers, directors, and actors suffered from the Red Scare as they found themselves "blacklisted," or branded as communists, and unable to get work.

Even while the U.S. faced fears of communism, the country focused on building up its own capitalist system; in 1946, American automakers produced two million cars.

had taken place during the war to provide increased amounts of rubber and other materials for the Allied war effort. After the war, the country, which had been ruled by dictator Getúlio Vargas since 1930, approved a new constitution that set up regular elections. In Argentina, which had remained neutral throughout the war, newly elected president Juan Perón began an industrialization program, constructing steel and textile mills, among other factories. His reforms were initially successful, and Argentineans found themselves the beneficiaries of rising wages.

In contrast, on the Caribbean island of Cuba, citizens endured continued government corruption, which had been widespread throughout various Cuban administrations since the country had been granted independence from U.S. occupation in 1902. Officials skimmed funds from the country's treasury, and organized crime ran rampant on the island, controlling everything from tourism to prostitution. A huge gap opened between the very wealthy in the country and the poor, who suffered from the high prices of goods.

Across the Atlantic, in Africa, where many lands were still colonies of the British and French, World War II had

"When a great democracy is destroyed, it will not be because of enemies from without but rather because of enemies from within. . . . At war's end, we were physically the strongest nation on Earth and, at least potentially, the most powerful intellectually and morally. . . . The reason why we find ourselves in a position of impotency is not because our only powerful, potential enemy has sent men to invade our shores, but rather because of the traitorous actions of those who have been treated so well by this nation. . . . In my opinion, the State Department . . . is thoroughly infested with communists."

JOSEPH MCCARTHY, U.S. Senator, February 1950

8

While Cuban sugar producers grew wealthy from increased trade after World War II, the country's poor lived in crude shacks and suffered from the rising prices of many goods.

Although Warsaw, Poland, had once been a magnificent city, by the end of World War II, more than 85 percent of its buildings had been destroyed by the Germans.

galvanized a new move for independence. Inspired by Ethiopia, which, with the help of Britain, had overthrown Italian invaders during the war, people in countries from Algeria to South Africa began to work with renewed vigor for the right to rule their own land.

Meanwhile, to the north of Africa, nearly the entire continent of Europe lay in shambles. Millions of homes in countries from Britain and Italy to Germany and Poland had been destroyed during the course of the war, leaving countless citizens homeless. Transportation systems in nations across Europe had been reduced to rubble. With thousands of factories damaged—and millions of workers killed—during the war, the production levels of many countries fell dramatically. Farm produc-

The target of 229 Allied bombing raids, the city of Duisburg, Germany, was severely damaged during World War II, with many industries and residences ruined.

tion also fell sharply, resulting in the near-starvation of an estimated 100 million Europeans by 1945.

On the far eastern edge of Europe, in the vast expanse of the Soviet Union, the war had had devastating effects as well. More than 32,000 factories, 100,000 farms, and 71,000 entire towns and villages had been destroyed following the German invasion of the country in 1941. More significantly, 27 million Soviets lay dead as a result of the war—the highest death toll suffered by any nation.

For the 167 million Soviets who had survived, life was bleak. Since 1922, the Soviet Union, officially known as the Union of Soviet Socialist Republics, or USSR, had been a communist country, under which the government owned all businesses. Ideally, communism was supposed to make everyone equal and eliminate

poverty, but in practice, most Soviets found themselves living in poor conditions, suffering from shortages of food and other necessities, while the country's government leaders lived in luxury. Besides enduring physical hardship, many in the Soviet Union lived in perpetual fear, as freedom of speech was severely limited; those who criticized the government swiftly found themselves exiled to prison camps or executed.

Despite the devastation and hardship wrought by World War II, the Soviet Union quickly moved into the role of the only superpower in the Eastern Hemisphere after the war, retaining a huge, powerful army. Under the direction of ruthless dictator Joseph Stalin, the country used the period immediately following the war to begin to establish communist control in Eastern Europe, with the goal of creating a buffer between the

In the Soviet Union, World War II was known as the Great Patriotic War, and propaganda posters declared "Glory to all soldiers of the Red Army!"

In the aftermath of World War II, the U.S. feared that poverty in European nations devastated by the war would enable support for communism to take root. Thus, the U.S. instituted a program known as the Marshall Plan to provide financial aid to help rebuild the continent. Although a few Eastern European nations expressed interest in applying for Marshall Plan aid, they withdrew their interest under Soviet threat. As a result, all Marshall Plan aid went to Western Europe, widening the divide between the Soviet-influenced and U.S.-influenced spheres.

As the U.S. and Soviet Union vied for control in Europe after World War II, young East Germans marched through the streets carrying posters honoring Joseph Stalin.

Soviet dictator Joseph Stalin

Soviet Union and Western Europe, thus preventing the country from ever again being invaded by the West as it had been by Nazi Germany.

One of the first nations to fall under Soviet control was the eastern portion of defeated Germany. In the months before the war's end, when it was obvious that the Allies would be victorious, the four powers had agreed to temporarily split Germany among them after the war, with each Allied nation occupying a specific zone of the country. Although the other three Allied nations—the U.S., Britain, and France—allowed a democratic government to take shape in their zones of occupation in western Germany,

the Soviet Union installed a communist government in eastern Germany.

In the Eastern European countries of Poland, Romania, Bulgaria, Hungary, and Czechoslovakia, the Soviet Union also worked toward setting up pro-Soviet communist governments. In most cases, the Soviets worked carefully to set up governments that would last. First, they positioned local communists in important government offices, such as minister of justice; then, by means of threats, imprisonment, and even murder, they removed political opponents. Finally, after staging large-scale propaganda campaigns to drum up support for communism, the Soviet Union proclaimed the nation

"What can be surprising in the fact that the Soviet Union, in a desire to ensure its security for the future, tries to [ensure that Eastern Europe] should have governments whose relations to the Soviet Union are loyal? How can one, without having lost one's reason, qualify these peaceful aspirations of the Soviet Union as 'expansionist tendencies' of our government? . . . The influence of the communists grew because during the hard years of the mastery of fascism in Europe, communists showed themselves to be reliable, daring, and self-sacrificing fighters against fascist regimes for the liberty of peoples."

JOSEPH STALIN, Soviet dictator, 1946

a communist republic. The Soviets'
tactics worked. Within two years of
the end of the war, every country in
Eastern Europe, with the exception
of Czechoslovakia, had a communist
government in place.

As the nations of the West—
especially the U.S. and Britain—
watched the Soviet Union quickly
gain influence over more and more
Eastern European nations, their
anxiety grew. These democratic
countries, in which everyone had
a say in the government, had been
suspicious of communism since the
Russian Revolution of 1917 had led
to the formation of the Soviet Union as
the world's first communist nation. The
Bolsheviks, the communist leaders of the
revolution, had made clear that
their ultimate goal was to instigate
communist revolutions in countries
all around the world, bringing

In 1956, an anti-communist uprising in
Hungary was met with Soviet tanks.

In some places, such as Germany, the "iron curtain" between East and West took the tangible form of barbed wire fences, separating families and friends.

capitalism and democracy to an end everywhere. Now, in the aftermath of World War II, the West's worst fears of a Soviet desire for communist domination seemed to be realized. The Soviets, for their part, were suspicious of the West as well, and had been since 1918, when the U.S., Britain, and France had intervened to support anti-communist forces in a civil war that followed the Russian Revolution.

Although the Soviet Union and the U.S. had fought as allies against a common enemy during World War II, tensions between the two nations were higher than ever in the months after their shared wartime victory. Soon, the two countries were thinking of each other as enemies, rather than allies. In March 1946, speaking at a college in Missouri, former British Prime Minister Winston Churchill told his American audience that an "iron curtain" had descended across Europe, dividing the continent between Western democracies and the Eastern communist bloc. He seemed to be announcing the start of the Cold War.

"From Stettin in the Baltic to Trieste in the Adriatic, an iron curtain has descended across the continent. Behind that line lie all the capitals of the ancient states of central and eastern Europe. Warsaw, Berlin, Prague, Vienna, Budapest, Belgrade, Bucharest, and Sofia, all these famous cities and populations around them lie in the Soviet sphere and all are subject, in one form or another, not only to Soviet influence but to a very high and increasing measure of control from Moscow. . . . This is certainly not the liberated Europe we fought to build up."

WINSTON CHURCHILL, former British prime minister, March 5, 1946

19

20

As Western fears of Soviet expansion continued to intensify in the early postwar years, the U.S. adopted a new foreign policy known as containment. Its basic objective was to prevent the spread of Soviet influence past Eastern Europe. The centerpiece of this policy was the Truman Doctrine, which pledged U.S. military and financial support to any nation in the world resisting an attempted communist takeover.

The first real test of the Truman Doctrine occurred in 1948 in the city of Berlin. By that year, the three Western Allies had decided to merge together their zones of occupation throughout Germany— including in Berlin, which, although deep inside Soviet-occupied eastern Germany, had also been divided into four occupation zones. In order to strengthen western Germany's economy and bring inflation, or sustained price increases, under control, the Western Allies announced the introduction of a new currency in western Germany and West Berlin. Stalin, who favored keeping Germany weak so that it could never again invade his country, was angered by the move and quickly set up a blockade of West Berlin, preventing all traffic— including vehicles carrying needed supplies—from entering the city. His plan was to starve the two and a half million people of West Berlin until the Western Allies relinquished control of all of Berlin to the Soviet Union. Instead, the U.S. and Britain began a massive airlift of supplies into the city. For 11 months, more than 5,000 tons (4,500 t) of food, fuel, medicine, and other necessities were flown into West Berlin each day.

AN ICY RELATIONSHIP

With American and British supply planes landing at a rate of one a minute, the people of West Berlin had enough rations to see them through the Soviet blockade.

Finally, on May 12, 1949, the Soviet Union lifted the blockade, winning the U.S. worldwide respect for its determination to stand up to Soviet aggression.

The next major Cold War achievement would go to the Soviets, however. In August 1949, the Soviet Union test-detonated its first atomic weapon. With that, the Soviet Union and the U.S.—which had developed the atomic bomb in 1945 and used it against the Japanese cities of Hiroshima and Nagasaki to end World War II—were on equal footing in an arms race that would come to dominate the entire Cold War period.

Less than a year after the Soviet Union became a nuclear power, the Cold War escalated into open warfare when the armies of communist North Korea, encouraged by Stalin, invaded democratic South Korea. The U.S. and the United Nations

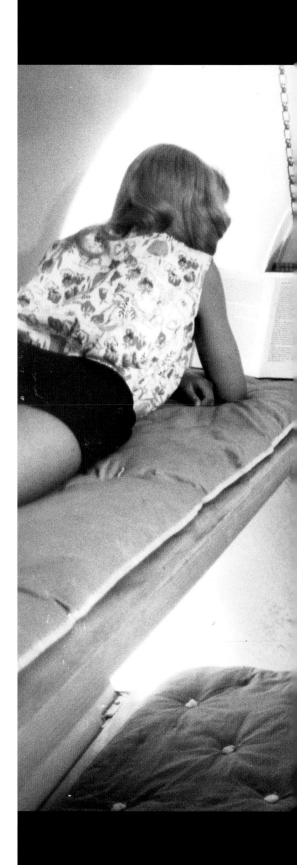

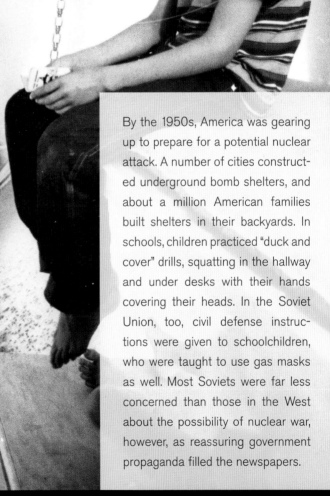

By the 1950s, America was gearing up to prepare for a potential nuclear attack. A number of cities constructed underground bomb shelters, and about a million American families built shelters in their backyards. In schools, children practiced "duck and cover" drills, squatting in the hallway and under desks with their hands covering their heads. In the Soviet Union, too, civil defense instructions were given to schoolchildren, who were taught to use gas masks as well. Most Soviets were far less concerned than those in the West about the possibility of nuclear war, however, as reassuring government propaganda filled the newspapers.

Backyard bomb shelters included bunks, emergency oxygen supplies, and water, as well as whatever comforts, such as radios and games, families added to them.

At the peak of the Vietnam War, more than 540,000 U.S. soldiers were in Vietnam, even while many Americans protested U.S. involvement in what they saw as a civil war.

sent troops to defend South Korea, and China, which had been taken over by communists in 1949, eventually joined the fight on the side of North Korea. Ultimately, the war reached a stalemate, and an armistice was signed in July 1953.

Soon after the end of the Korean War, the Soviet Union and the U.S. again found themselves supporting opposite sides in an escalating conflict in Southeast Asia. This time, the conflict was in Vietnam, where the Soviet-supported communist forces of North Vietnam and the Viet Cong (communist guerrilla fighters) opposed South Vietnam. Fearing that if South Vietnam fell to communism, it would begin a domino effect, bringing communism to all of Southeast Asia, the U.S. intervened, first (beginning in 1955) by sending advisers to train the South Vietnamese army and eventually (beginning in 1965) by sending hundreds of thousands of combat troops to Vietnam. The attempt to prevent the spread of communism into South Vietnam was ultimately unsuccessful, however. In 1973, after 58,000 U.S. soldiers had died, American troops were withdrawn from Vietnam; two years later, North Vietnam overran the South.

"The superpowers often behave like two heavily armed blind men feeling their way around a room, each believing himself in a mortal peril from the other whom he assumes to have perfect vision. . . . Of course, over time, even two blind men can do enormous damage to each other, not to speak of the room."

HENRY KISSINGER, U.S. secretary of state under Presidents Nixon and Ford, 1979

Even as these "hot" wars were taking place, the nuclear arms race between the U.S. and the Soviet Union continued. By 1953, both nations had developed the hydrogen bomb, a weapon 1,000 times more powerful than the first atomic bombs. As the two nations focused on creating more and more destructive weapons, both also set their sights on developing planes and missiles to transport their weapons to enemy targets as quickly as possible. In 1957, the Soviet Union launched *Sputnik I*, the world's first artificial satellite. The event stunned Americans, who realized that a missile powerful enough to send a satellite into space could also launch nuclear warheads from the Soviet Union to their homes.

While the U.S. raced to catch up with Soviet space technology, the Cold War began to intensify in East Germany, where thousands of

At the 1958 World's Fair in Brussels, Belgium, the Soviet Union eagerly displayed evidence
of its latest technological achievements, including space satellites.

Although the Berlin Wall was closely watched by armed guards, thousands of East Germans risked their lives attempting to cross it. In 1962, Peter Fechter, an 18-year-old bricklayer, was shot as he scaled the wall. As he bled to death, West Berliners begged the American soldiers at a nearby checkpoint to rescue him, but the soldiers had orders not to intervene—the young man was on the eastern side of the wall, in Soviet-controlled territory, and American interference threatened to ignite a deadly international confrontation. Fechter soon died, becoming one of more than 200 people to be killed in attempted wall crossings during the structure's nearly three decades of existence.

At the orders of the East German government, and with the approval of the Soviet Union, East German troops and workers built the 96-mile-long (155 km) Berlin Wall.

East German citizens longed to escape to West Germany. With barbed-wire fences and armed guards along most of the border between eastern and western Europe, however, East Germans had little chance of making it to the West. Their only hope was to travel to East Berlin, slip into the western section of the city, and either stay there or seek a flight to another West German city. Millions chose this route; by 1961, nearly three million people had fled from East Germany, taking with them vitally needed skills in medicine, engineering, and other professions. In order to stop the mass exodus from the East, in August 1961, the East German government constructed a 12-foot-high (3.7 m) wall around West Berlin.

Only a year after the erection of the Berlin Wall, the most dangerous crisis of the Cold War arose when a U.S. spy plane flying over Cuba discovered Soviet nuclear missile installations on the island, which had declared itself communist in 1961. U.S. President John F. Kennedy demanded that the Soviets remove the missiles, which were capable of launching nuclear warheads to nearly any city

"Freedom has many difficulties and democracy is not perfect, but we have never had to put a wall up to keep our people in, to prevent them from leaving us. . . . While the [Berlin Wall] is the most obvious and vivid demonstration of the failures of the communist system, for all the world to see, we take no satisfaction in it, for it is . . . an offense not only against history but an offense against humanity, separating families, dividing husbands and wives and brothers and sisters, and dividing a people who wish to be joined together."

JOHN F. KENNEDY, U.S. president, June 26, 1963

29

During the tensest periods of the Cold War, even the slightest clashes threatened to spark full-scale conflicts. In one incident in 1961, an American diplomat named E. Allan Lightner was not allowed to cross into East Berlin because he refused to show his passport. Since Allied officials were supposed to be able to cross the border freely, U.S. soldiers arrived and escorted the diplomat into East Berlin. After a similar episode a few days later, 10 U.S. tanks were pulled up near the border crossing; 10 Soviet tanks quickly pulled up across from them. Following an uneasy 16-hour showdown, both sides withdrew their tanks with no shots having been fired.

With only 240 yards (220 m) separating U.S. and Soviet tanks in Berlin in October 1961, leaders on both sides feared that a jumpy soldier might accidentally trigger a shootout.

in the U.S. The U.S. also began a naval blockade of Cuba, seeking to prevent Soviet ships from reaching the island, and prepared its own nuclear weapons for a retaliatory strike upon the Soviet Union. Finally, after 13 days of negotiations, Soviet dictator Nikita Khrushchev agreed to remove the missiles in return for a U.S. promise not to invade Cuba and to withdraw its nuclear weapons from Turkey.

After the Cuban Missile Crisis, tensions between the two superpowers began to ease slightly, and by the end of the 1960s, they were pursuing a policy of *détente* (French for "relaxation of tensions"). Détente lasted for a decade, but it fell apart in December 1979 when the Soviet Union invaded Afghanistan in order to support the country's communist government against opposition fighters. Infuriated, the U.S. provided millions of dollars in aid to the resistance fighters, who inflicted 13,000 Soviet casualties. The U.S. also soon began a massive military buildup, which was quickly matched by the Soviet Union. By 1989—when the Soviet Union withdrew from Afghanistan, leaving the country in the grips of a civil war—there were 50,000 nuclear weapons in

31

"You can regard us with distrust, but in any case you can be perfectly [confident] . . . that we are of sound mind and understand perfectly well that if we attack you, you will respond in the same way. . . . This shows that we are normal people, that we understand and evaluate the situation correctly. . . . Only lunatics or suicides, who themselves want to perish and destroy the whole world before they die, could [plan to attack you]. We, however, want to live and do not at all want to destroy your country."

NIKITA KHRUSHCHEV, Soviet dictator, letter to President Kennedy during the Cuban Missile Crisis, October 26, 1962

Soviet dictator Mikhail Gorbachev

the world, enough to destroy civilization many times over.

Even as both sides continued to build up their nuclear weapons stockpiles, however, a more hopeful period in U.S.-Soviet relations was beginning. In 1985, Mikhail Gorbachev became General Secretary of the Soviet Communist Party (and thereby dictator of the Soviet Union) and announced two far-reaching reforms: *perestroika* (economic restructuring) and *glasnost* (political openness). In order to implement these reforms, Gorbachev knew that the Soviet Union would have to cut back on its military spending by bringing an end to the arms race with the U.S. In a series of four summit meetings between 1985 and 1988, Gorbachev and U.S. President Ronald Reagan began new

arms control talks. Then, in December 1988, Gorbachev announced to the UN that he was committed to "freedom of choice" for the countries of Eastern Europe, meaning that they would no longer be forced to retain communist governments.

With Gorbachev's announcement, countries throughout Eastern Europe began to make moves to install democratic governments. Most dramatic was the change in East Germany, which announced on November 9, 1989, that citizens would be allowed to cross the Berlin Wall—and to remain permanently in West Germany if they wished. That night, German citizens began to dismantle the wall, hacking off pieces of the hated structure. The Cold War was effectively at an end.

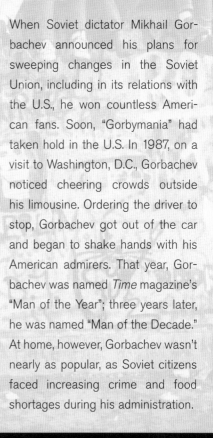

When Soviet dictator Mikhail Gorbachev announced his plans for sweeping changes in the Soviet Union, including in its relations with the U.S., he won countless American fans. Soon, "Gorbymania" had taken hold in the U.S. In 1987, on a visit to Washington, D.C., Gorbachev noticed cheering crowds outside his limousine. Ordering the driver to stop, Gorbachev got out of the car and began to shake hands with his American admirers. That year, Gorbachev was named *Time* magazine's "Man of the Year"; three years later, he was named "Man of the Decade." At home, however, Gorbachev wasn't nearly as popular, as Soviet citizens faced increasing crime and food shortages during his administration.

In October 1989, Mikhail Gorbachev visited East Germany, where he promoted change; by November, joyful Germans were celebrating the opening of the Berlin Wall.

Although the fall of the Berlin Wall in effect marked the end of the Cold War, the remarkable events set in motion by Mikhail Gorbachev's dramatic speech to the UN continued to unfold. By the end of 1989, nearly every Eastern European country once under Soviet control had turned from the system of communism. Surprisingly, in almost every nation—aside from Romania, where the country's former communist ruler was executed—the change in government occurred peacefully.

In the Soviet Union itself, Gorbachev's announcement of "freedom of choice" had unexpected results, as the various republics of the Soviet Union began to call for independence. Gorbachev, whose goal was to restructure the Soviet Union, not eliminate it, at first resisted such moves through political pressure and even armed force. Still, more and more of the Soviet Union's 15 republics clamored for independence. Then, in August 1991, while Gorbachev was away at his vacation home, hard-line communists, who thought Gorbachev had gone too far with his reforms, placed him under house arrest and attempted to take control in Moscow.

The attempted coup failed, however, as Boris Yeltsin, the president of the Soviet Union's largest republic—Russia—urged his people to resist the takeover. Three days later, when Gorbachev returned to Moscow, he found that Yeltsin now had the support of the Soviet people. With his hold on the country weakened, Gorbachev was unable to prevent the Soviet republics from declaring

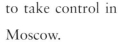

A NEW WORLD

In Czechoslovakia, peaceful demonstrations during the bloodless "Velvet Revolution" of 1989 led to the end of communism and the election of Václav Havel as president.

Even before the collapse of the Soviet Union, many Russians searched notices on bulletin boards for affordable housing; conditions worsened after the Soviet Union fell apart.

their independence, and several did so. In December 1991, the Soviet Union was officially dissolved, and, with no country to rule, Gorbachev resigned.

With the dissolution of the Soviet Union—and the change to democratic governments in the countries of Eastern Europe—the U.S. celebrated a long-sought victory over communism and emerged as the world's sole superpower. Yet the Cold War had not been without its costs, even in the West. The U.S. had accumulated a significant federal debt as it dedicated huge amounts of money to building up its nuclear arsenals throughout the Cold War. By 1989, the country's total federal debt (owed to individuals holding U.S. treasury notes and bonds, such as savings bonds) had reached $2.6 trillion. The cost of the Cold War was measured not only in dollars, but in human lives as well. Although the Cold War never involved a direct confrontation between the U.S. and the Soviet Union, the Korean and Vietnam Wars had resulted in the deaths of more than 100,000 Americans.

In the former countries of the Soviet Union, the end of the Cold War brought independence and greater freedoms, but not necessarily peace and prosperity. In Russia, most citizens found themselves even worse off than they had been under communist rule. As in many of the post-communist nations, the government attempted to institute rapid

Although Russians stood in line for goods in the late 1980s, only 1.5 percent of the
population lived in poverty; by 1993, about 40 percent of Russians were poverty-stricken.

reforms, selling state-owned industries to private parties. For workers in businesses that no one wanted, this meant almost instant unemployment, as the businesses were shut down. Even those who were able to hold on to their jobs had difficulties making ends meet, as the government, too weak to collect taxes, couldn't afford to pay soldiers and other state employees for months at a time. In 1999, President Boris Yeltsin resigned. Under Yeltsin's democratically elected successor, Vladimir Putin, Russian citizens began to enjoy a slightly better standard of living, and store shelves were fully stocked for the first time in years.

Many of the countries of Eastern Europe suffered similar difficulties as they worked to establish non-communist governments following the end of the Cold War. In Germany, the reunification of East and West brought about rising unemployment, as many out-of-date East German factories were closed. In Albania, which even before the end of the Cold War had been the poorest country in Europe, unemployment skyrocketed to 51 percent. In Bosnia and other successor states of Yugoslavia (which broke apart in 1991), old hatreds

"Last week, I was standing in a terrible line for meat. . . . I was standing there for five and a half hours. We had lines . . . [before], but they were not so big and we stood in those lines not for everything. But now we have lines for everything. Beginning with meat and shoes and ending with matches and salt. We stand for rice, for sugar, for butter, for thread, for deodorants. . . . Every country helps us. We already openly asked for alms [charity], and we accept them very calmly. We forget about one very good word. Pride. I am ashamed of my country."

14-year-old Soviet high school student, February 14, 1991

39

Brutal ethnic conflicts led more than two million Bosnian refugees—about half of the country's population—to flee from their homes in the early 1990s.

ignited into bloody clashes, as members of the Serb ethnic group sought to expel or kill non-Serbs throughout much of the region, sparking a conflict that resulted in hundreds of thousands of deaths in the 1990s.

Other countries fared better. In Bulgaria, the privatization of industry went well, and food supplies were plentiful. Privatization was successful in Hungary as well, and many of the nation's businesses began to partner with Western enterprises. And in the Czech Republic—newly created by the division of Czechoslovakia into the Czech Republic and Slovakia—unemployment rates were lower even than those in the U.S.

Eventually, many former Eastern bloc countries were invited to become members of formerly Western-only organizations, including the European Union, an economic and political alliance between European nations, and the North Atlantic Treaty Organization (NATO), a military alliance between the U.S., Canada, and many European countries. Although Russia itself has not become an official member of NATO, it participates in the new NATO-Russia Council, discussing many international

"Nobody 'won' the Cold War. . . . It greatly overstrained the economic resources of both countries, leaving them both, by the end of the 1980s, confronted with heavy financial, social, and—in the case of the Russians— political problems neither had anticipated. . . . The fact that in Russia's case these changes were long desired on principle by most of us does not alter the fact that they came . . . upon a population little prepared for them, thus creating new problems of the greatest seriousness for Russia, her neighbors, and the rest of us—problems to which, as yet, none of us have found effective answers."

GEORGE F. KENNAN, American diplomat and historian, 1996

41

issues with NATO members. While tensions between the U.S. and Russia have not completely disappeared—in 2001, for example, each country expelled 50 of the other country's suspected spies—they have not again approached the levels of tension experienced during the Cold War, when the world seemed to be constantly on the brink of nuclear disaster.

Despite this fact, some people argue that the end of the Cold War didn't necessarily make the world a safer place. During the Cold War, they say, a kind of stability emerged, as countries pledged their loyalty to either the West or to the communist bloc. Although the U.S. and the Soviet Union often intervened in regional conflicts, seeking to gain an advantage over the other, each was always careful not to push the other country too far. In this way, regional conflicts were kept from escalating out of control. With the absence of this superpower rivalry to shape world events, some fear that there is now nothing to rein in such regional conflicts.

"Today, every inhabitant of this planet must contemplate the day when this planet may no longer be habitable. Every man, woman, and child lives under a nuclear sword of Damocles, hanging by the slenderest of threads, capable of being cut at any moment by accident or miscalculation or by madness. The weapons of war must be abolished before they abolish us. The mere existence of modern weapons . . . is a source of horror and discord and distrust."

JOHN F. KENNEDY, U.S. president, September 25, 1961

Others point out that even with the end of the Cold War, the world is by no means free of the nuclear threat. Although many nuclear weapons on both sides have been dismantled in

I CERTIFY THAT the foregoing is a true copy of the North Atlantic Treaty signed at Washington on April 4, 1949 in the English and French languages, the signed original of which is deposited in the archives of the Government of the United States of America.

IN TESTIMONY WHEREOF, I, DEAN ACHESON, Secretary of State of the United States of America, have hereunto caused the seal of the Department of State to be affixed and my name subscribed by the Authentication Officer of the said Department, at the city of Washington, in the District of Columbia, this fourth day of April, 1949.

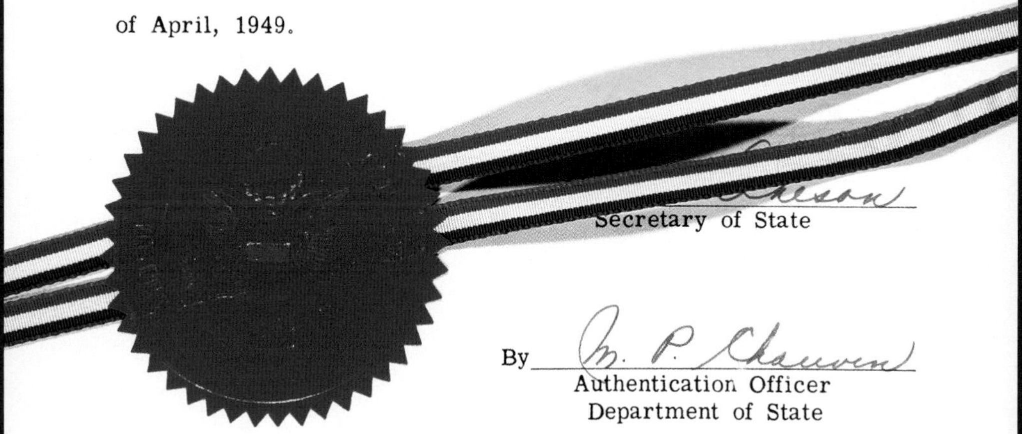

Secretary of State

By M. P. Chauvin
Authentication Officer
Department of State

The 26 nations—including many formerly communist countries—that today belong to the North Atlantic Treaty Organization pledge to defend one another from outside attack.

Although the main conflicts of the Cold War took place in Europe, Asia, and Cuba, the rivalry between the U.S. and the Soviet Union also stretched to other parts of the globe. In Africa, the U.S. and the Soviet Union backed opposite sides in civil wars in a number of nations, including Angola and Lebanon. In Central and South America, the U.S. worked to overthrow pro-Soviet leaders and install pro-American governments in countries such as Chile, Nicaragua, and Grenada. And in the Middle East, the U.S. supported democratic Israel in conflicts against Soviet-backed Arab nations.

Today, violence continues to rock Israel, where Palestinian suicide bombers regularly kill civilians; both the U.S. and Russia are involved in the Middle East peace process.

the years since the end of the Cold War, today's nuclear arsenals hold a combined 30,000 weapons with a total destructive force equal to that of eight million tons (7.3 million t) of TNT. With so many nuclear weapons remaining in the world, there is widespread fear that they may fall into the hands of terrorists. In fact, with the breakdown of law and order in Russia in the aftermath of the Cold War, there were at least 21 attempted thefts from Russian nuclear facilities in the 1990s. In order to prevent terrorists from getting their hands on nuclear materials, the U.S. today spends nearly $1 billion a year to help Russia improve security at its nuclear weapons sites.

Such actions aren't enough for some people, who say that the world won't be free of the threat of nuclear warfare until all of the planet's nuclear weapons are destroyed. A step toward this goal was taken with the Nuclear Non-Proliferation Treaty, introduced in 1968 and since signed by 188 countries. The majority of the countries that have signed the treaty have done so as non-nuclear powers, agreeing not to pursue the development of nuclear weapons. Only five countries—the U.S., Britain, Russia, China, and France—are allowed under the terms of the treaty to possess such

"Nuclear warfare is an utter folly, even from the narrowest point of view of self-interest. To spread ruin, misery, and death throughout one's own country as well as that of the enemy is the act of madmen. . . . The question every human being must ask is 'can man survive?'"

BERTRAND RUSSELL, founder of the British Campaign for Nuclear Disarmament, 1950s

45

weapons (although a handful of countries today remain outside of the treaty and some, such as Pakistan and India, have nuclear weapons). Yet, even the five legal nuclear nations, in signing the treaty, have agreed to make efforts to reduce their stockpiles of nuclear weapons and eventually work toward complete nuclear disarmament. With these measures, it is hoped that the nuclear tensions of the Cold War will someday become a distant memory, read about in books but never experienced by another generation of Americans, Russians, or world citizens.

Although the conclusion of the Cold War brought an end to repressive communist regimes in countries throughout Eastern Europe and Asia, it didn't bring a complete end to communism. In China, a communist government continues to flourish in the post-Cold War world, and many believe that China is poised to someday become a superpower. In Cuba, Vietnam, and North Korea, communist regimes also remain in place. Today, tensions between the world's communist nations and the U.S. occasionally flare up; relations with North Korea are especially strained, since the country withdrew from the Nuclear Non-Proliferation Treaty in 2003 and in 2005 announced that it had developed nuclear weapons.

Although some scholars fear the prospect of a new Cold War with China—whose youths

BIBLIOGRAPHY

Greer, Thomas, and Gavin Lewis. *A Brief History of the Western World.*
Belmont, Cal.: Thomson Wadsworth, 2005.

Hatt, Christine. *The End of the Cold War.*
Milwaukee: World Almanac Library, 2002.

Isaacs, Jeremy, and Taylor Downing. *Cold War: An Illustrated History, 1945–1991.*
New York: Little, Brown and Company, 1998.

Kort, Michael. *The Cold War.* Brookfield, Conn.: Millbrook Press, 1994.

Ross, Stewart. *The Causes of the Cold War.*
Milwaukee: World Almanac Library, 2002.

Speakman, Jay. *Opposing Viewpoints: The Cold War.*
San Diego: Greenhaven, 2001.

Winkler, Allan. *The Cold War: A History in Documents.*
New York: Oxford University Press, 2000.

INDEX